THE SOLAR SYSTEM

Chris Cooper

SCIENCE
FACT FILES

THE SOLAR SYSTEM

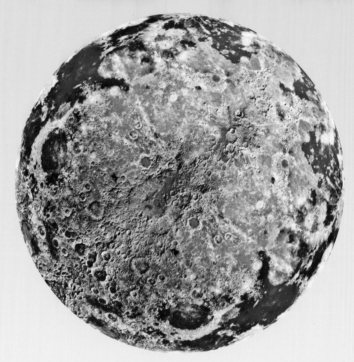

Chris Cooper

RAINTREE
STECK-VAUGHN
PUBLISHERS

A Harcourt Company

Austin · New York
www.steck-vaughn.com

Produced by Roger Coote Publishing

Published by Raintree Steck-Vaughn, an imprint of Steck-Vaughn Company

Design and typesetting	Victoria Webb
Commissioning Editor	Lisa Edwards
Editor	Roger Goddard-Coote
Picture Researcher	Lynda Lines
Illustrator	Alex Pang

Raintree Steck-Vaughn Staff:

Editor	Kathy DeVico
Project Manager	Max Brinkmann

Library of Congress Cataloging-in-Publication Data

Cooper, Christopher (Christopher E.)
  The solar system / Chris Cooper.
    p. cm. — (Science fact files)
  Includes bibliographical references and index.
  Summary: Examines the characteristics of the planets and other heavenly bodies in our solar system.
  ISBN 0-7398-1006-5
  1. Solar system—Juvenile literature. [1. Solar system.] I. Title. II. Series.

  QB501.3 .C66 2001
  523.2 21—dc21   99-044322

Pages 2–3: The rings of the giant gas planet Saturn are a swarm of millions of tiny moons, made of rock and ice.
Title page picture: The far side of the Moon

We are grateful to the following for permission to reproduce photographs:
Science Photo Library 12–13 (NOAO), 14 top (NASA), 14 center (NASA), 17 (European Space Agency), 18 top (U.S. Geological Survey), 19 bottom (NASA), 23 (NASA), 27 top (NASA), 29 (David A Hardy), 32 top (Detlev Van Ravenswaay), 32 bottom (François Gohier), 33 (Pekka Parviainen), 34 (European Space Agency).
Remaining photos are courtesy of Digital Vision.

The statistics given in this book are the most up to date available at the time of going to press.

Printed in Hong Kong

0 1 2 3 4 5 6 7 8 9 WKT 05 04 03 02 01 00

CONTENTS

27.14 (19.00)

4-16-04

INTRODUCTION

The solar system consists of the Sun and the many **planets** and other bodies that circle it. These include Earth and eight other planets, thousands of **comets** and **asteroids**, and countless millions of rocks and grains of dust. The first four planets, moving outward from the Sun, are rocky and small. They are only a few thousand kilometers across. Earth is one of these. The next four planets are known as gas giants. They are made of hydrogen, helium, and other gases, and are tens of thousands of kilometers across. The outermost known planet, Pluto, is believed to be another rocky planet.

Though Pluto is the outermost of the known planets, it is not the farthest member of the solar system. The outer limit of the solar system is far beyond Pluto. It is an unseen cloud of "sleeping comets," halfway between the Sun and the nearest **stars**.

The whole solar system belongs to an enormous system of stars, gas, and dust called the Galaxy, which contains billions of stars. Circling many of these stars there must be other planetary systems like our own solar system.

Gravitation

The solar system is held together by gravitation. This is a force with which every particle of matter in the universe pulls on every other particle. Earth's gravitational pull keeps you held to the ground, and

Our galaxy contains 100 billion stars, together with gas and dust, in a swirling spiral 100,000 light years across.

it holds artificial **satellites** and the Moon in their paths around Earth. Because it contains so much matter, the Sun has a huge gravitational pull, which is strong enough to keep all the other members of the solar system from escaping into distant space.

All the planets except Mercury and Venus have natural satellites, or moons, circling them. The moons are prevented from escaping by the planets' own gravitational pulls. Earth has just one satellite, the Moon. However, each of the gas giants has a family of them, like a miniature solar system.

The major planets of the solar system

Sun

Key
1 Mercury
2 Venus
3 Earth
4 Mars
5 Jupiter
6 Saturn
7 Uranus
8 Neptune
9 Pluto

Key

1	Mercury	8	Neptune
2	Venus	9	Pluto
3	Earth	10	Sun
4	Mars	11	Asteroids
5	Jupiter	12	Halley's comet
6	Saturn	13	Comet Swift-Tuttle
7	Uranus	14	Kuiper Belt

The paths of the planets and satellites are called **orbits**. These orbits are **elliptical** (oval, or egg-shaped). A planet travels fastest in the part of its orbit that is closest to the Sun, and slower farther away. The larger a planet's orbit, the longer it takes to travel around the Sun.

Different Worlds

Humans have not yet landed on any other planet or satellite except for the Moon. However, astronomers have found out a great deal about the planets from observations made with their telescopes and with unmanned space probes. They know that the planets of the solar system are very different from one another. For example, some are hotter than boiling water, while others are far colder than ice. In the future, as space travelers explore the solar system, we shall find out much more.

 FACT FILE

SOLAR SYSTEM DATA

Diameter (billion kilometers/miles):	14.75/9.17
Distance from center of Galaxy:	30,000 light years
Speed at which solar system moves around the center of the Galaxy:	220 kilometers/ 137 miles per second
Number of major planets:	9
Number of known planetary satellites:	64

Note: A **light year** is the distance light travels in 1 year; it is equal to 9.46 trillion kilometers (5.88 trillion miles).

The top diagram shows the inner solar system, from the Sun out to the asteroid belt. The bottom diagram shows the outer solar system. The planets (except Pluto) and the asteroids move in almost the same plane, but the orbits of many comets are tilted.

BIRTH OF THE SOLAR SYSTEM

1. The solar system began to form about 4.5 billion years ago, when a huge, swirling cloud of gas and dust was pulled together by its own gravity.

2. The Sun began to glow in the center of the cloud. Around it, "knots" of denser gas and dust formed. They would eventually become the planets.

Most astronomers believe that the solar system began 4.5 billion years ago, when a cloud of gas and dust, just one of many thousands in the Galaxy, began to shrink. It probably did so because it had been disturbed by the explosion of a nearby star. As the matter in the cloud crowded together, the gravitational attraction of each particle for every other particle became stronger. The gas and dust fell faster and faster toward the center, and the cloud began to spin faster and faster. As particles rubbed against each other, the gas and dust heated up. The heat increased the **pressure** at the center, which stopped the cloud from shrinking any more. As the temperature rose, nuclear reactions began in the heart of the cloud, turning hydrogen atoms into helium atoms. A new star had been born—the Sun.

In the Great Nebula in the constellation of Orion, new stars are being born. Some may have planets similar to those in the solar system.

The Planets Form

A strong solar "wind" blew from the Sun, consisting of fragments of atoms smashed by the intense heat. The **solar wind** and the intense sunlight blew away much of the gas from the central regions of the cloud. But grains of dust remained behind and collected together, pulled by their own gravitational attraction. Clumps of dust built up, collided to form larger clumps, attracted more dust by gravitation, and gradually built up into the rocky inner planets. This process may have taken about 100 million years.

In the cold, slow-moving gas and dust farther from the Sun, similar rocky bodies formed more quickly. The largest ones gathered huge **atmospheres** of hydrogen and helium around them. It took only about 10 million years for these giant planets to grow. Smaller bodies clustered around each one, forming families of satellites.

FUTURE FILE

OTHER PLANETARY SYSTEMS

It is very likely that most stars are born with their own systems of planets. But such planets are hard to see with even the most powerful telescopes because they are so far away. Only a few giant planets have been detected circling other stars.

Disks of dust, looking just as our solar system would have looked when it was only a few hundred million years old, have been discovered circling some nearby stars, such as the bright stars Vega and Fomalhaut. There are big holes near the middle of the disks, probably "swept clean" by young orbiting planets that we are not able to detect.

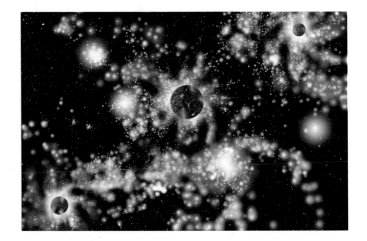

Leftover Matter

Some of the matter in the newly born solar system did not become part of the planets or satellites. It stayed independent, in the form of rocks and dust grains that pelted the planets for perhaps 600 million years. The bombardment gradually died away as the "cosmic dust" was used up, but we can still see the evidence today in the scarred surfaces of some planets and moons.

3. Small, rocky planets formed in the warm inner regions near the Sun. Huge gas giants formed in the cold outer regions.

4. Today the planets get light and heat from the Sun, which should continue to burn steadily for another 5 billion years.

THE SUN

In a hydrogen bomb, a few kilograms of hydrogen are turned into helium in a fraction of a second, releasing devastating quantities of energy. But in the Sun, 770 million tons of hydrogen are turned into helium every second. This outpouring of energy has been going on at much the same rate for the last 5 billion years. However, this enormous, long-lasting explosion is so far away that its heat and light do not destroy life on Earth—they make life possible.

The Sun's Core

At the center of the Sun, the temperature is 15 million°C (27 million°F), which means that particles of matter move around at very high speeds. The pressure is 300 billion times the pressure of Earth's atmosphere at sea level. In this environment atoms are broken down into pieces. The atom fragments are nuclei (the cores of the atoms) and electrons (which make up the outer parts). These fragments are constantly colliding with one another, and sometimes the hydrogen nuclei merge to form heavier nuclei. These also collide and from time to time merge. The final result of this sequence of reactions is to turn four hydrogen nuclei into one helium nucleus, releasing energy that keeps the Sun hot.

Energy travels from the center of the Sun to its surface and then into space as light, heat, and other kinds of radiation.

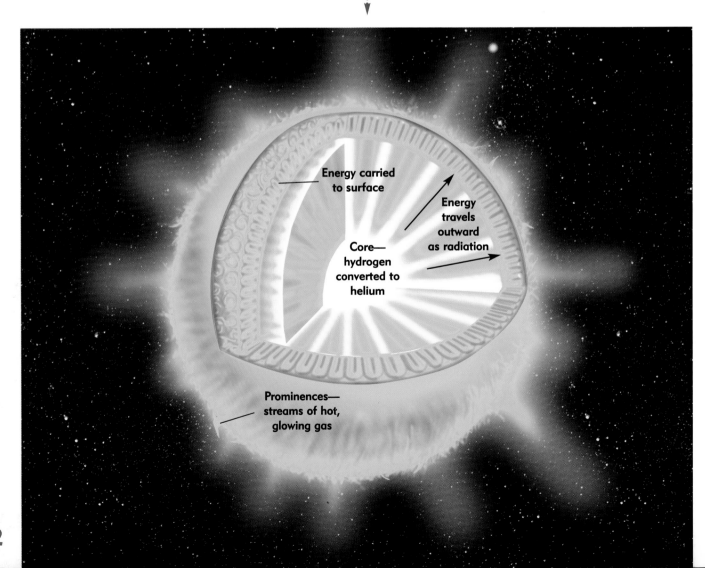

Energy carried to surface

Core—hydrogen converted to helium

Energy travels outward as radiation

Prominences—streams of hot, glowing gas

Sunspots appear as dark red patches in this picture of the Sun.

The Face of the Sun

The surface of the Sun seethes with violent activity. There are light and dark patches, hundreds or thousands of kilometers across, giving the surface a speckled appearance. (*Dark* here means less bright than the surroundings. All of the Sun's surface is blindingly bright.)

There are huge patches called sunspots, that are often bigger than Earth. They are relatively cool holes in the surface, where the Sun's intense **magnetic field** has broken through from the interior and slowed down the outward flow of heat. Sunspots build up in size and numbers. They reach a maximum every 11 years and then fade away.

Astronomers can find out how fast the Sun rotates by measuring how long sunspots take to move across the visible face of the Sun, or to reappear after vanishing around its far side. They find that, because the Sun is gaseous and not solid, different parts turn at different rates. The Sun takes slightly less than 4 weeks to rotate at its equator, but more than 5 weeks at its poles.

Sometimes explosions called flares are seen on the Sun. They last only minutes or hours and pour out visible light, X rays, and other **radiation**. The particles travel across space, and those that reach Earth can disturb radio communications and pose a danger to space travelers.

An enormous arch of glowing hydrogen gas erupts from the Sun's surface.

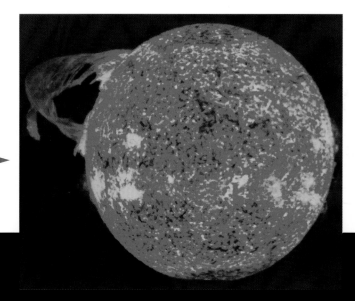

FACT FILE

SUN DATA

Rotation period:	26 days (equator); 37 days (poles)
Diameter at equator:	1,392,000 kilometers (865,000 miles)
Volume:	1,304,000 (Earth = 1)
Mass (Earth = 1):	329,000
Temperature:	5,500°C (9,932°F) at surface; approx. 15 million°C (27 million°F) at center
Density:	1.41 (water = 1)
Gravity at surface:	27.9 (Earth = 1)

MERCURY AND VENUS

The rocky surface of Mercury is scarred by meteoric craters, most of them billions of years old.

Two planets lie closer to the Sun than Earth does. One is Venus, which is almost the same size as Earth and covered in a thick atmosphere. Once it was thought that Venus was the planet most like Earth, and that there might be oceans and even life beneath the clouds. The other planet is tiny Mercury, the closest of all the planets to the Sun.

The Swift Planet
Mercury's **year**, or the time it takes to orbit the Sun, is just 88 Earth **days**. Yet the time it takes to rotate once is nearly 2 months, compared with 24 hours for Earth. The result is that daylight and nighttime on Mercury are each 88 days long.

Mercury's gravity is too weak to have held on to any atmosphere it may have had in the past. Its daytime side has no protection from the intense glare of the Sun, and the temperature can climb to over 420°C (788°F)—

Powerful winds circle the globe of Venus. The clouds consist of droplets of sulfuric acid.

TEST FILE

WATCHING MERCURY AND VENUS
Mercury and Venus appear in the western sky after sunset at certain times of the year (and in the eastern sky before sunrise at other times). This table gives the dates on which they appear highest in the west, up to the year 2005.

WARNING: Do not search for Mercury or Venus before the Sun is below the horizon.

Mercury
Mercury is visible for a few days before and after the dates shown here. It does not appear until about 40 minutes after sunset.

2000	February 14, June 8, October 6
2001	January 29, May 21, September 19
2002	January 12, May 4, August 31, December 26
2003	April 16, August 14, December 9
2004	March 29, July 26, November 20
2005	March 12, July 8, November 3

Venus
At its brightest, Venus looks brighter than any star. It appears in the evening sky every 19 months, but it is easily visible for at least 2 months before each of the dates given here. It is at its brightest 5 weeks after each date.

2000	(not visible)
2001	January 17
2002	August 22
2003	(not visible)
2004	March 29
2005	November 3

high enough to melt lead. But at midnight, the temperature drops to below –180°C (–356°F).

The surface of Mercury looks much the same as our Moon's surface. It is peppered with craters made by a barrage of **meteoroids** when the solar system was young. In places there are rocky plains, where large impacts caused molten lava to flood from beneath the surface.

The Hothouse Planet

Although Venus is farther away from the Sun than Mercury, its surface is even hotter, because the planet's heat is trapped by its dense atmosphere of carbon dioxide. Temperatures can reach 740°C (1,364°F).

The atmospheric pressure at the surface is about 90 times the air pressure on the surface of the Earth. The few spacecraft that have landed on Venus have soon been silenced by the crushing pressure and scorching heat, falling silent within an hour of landing.

Bright clouds made of droplets of sulfuric acid completely cover the planet, reflecting sunlight so strongly that Venus is the brightest object in our sky, apart from the Sun and Moon. Radar waves from orbiting spacecraft have penetrated the clouds to reveal mountains, craters, plains, and dead volcanoes. The Maxwell Mountains, for example, tower 17 kilometers (11 miles) high. This is nearly twice the height of Earth's Mount Everest.

The high mountains and rocky plains of Venus, as shown by radar scanning

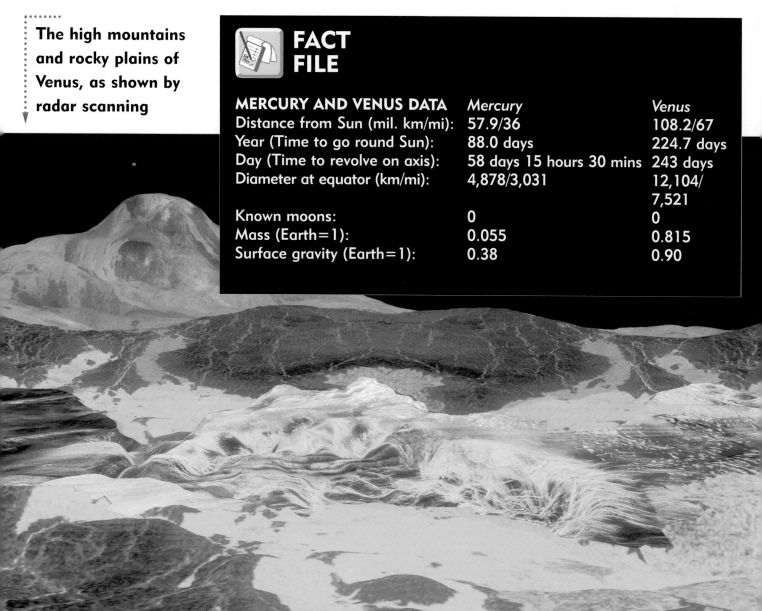

FACT FILE

MERCURY AND VENUS DATA	Mercury	Venus
Distance from Sun (mil. km/mi):	57.9/36	108.2/67
Year (Time to go round Sun):	88.0 days	224.7 days
Day (Time to revolve on axis):	58 days 15 hours 30 mins	243 days
Diameter at equator (km/mi):	4,878/3,031	12,104/ 7,521
Known moons:	0	0
Mass (Earth=1):	0.055	0.815
Surface gravity (Earth=1):	0.38	0.90

EARTH

Planet Earth is only slightly bigger than Venus. The two planets have similar **mass** and gravity. Yet conditions on the surface are very different. Earth's atmosphere is rich in nitrogen and oxygen, and it contains very little carbon dioxide. Water covers 74 percent of the surface. Living things flourish in the air, in the oceans, and on the land.

The Earth is farther from the Sun than Venus is, and its atmosphere contains much less carbon dioxide to trap the Sun's heat. As a result, Earth is much cooler than Venus. The average temperature on the surface is about 15°C (60°F).

Inside the Earth

Radioactive elements in Earth's interior, mainly uranium and thorium, probably produce the heat inside of the planet. The temperature at the center is at least 4,500°C (8,130°F). Scientists believe that the core consists of iron and nickel. Its outer parts are liquid, but the central core is squeezed into a solid form by the pressure of the overlying matter.

Outside the core is the mantle, which consists of rock and makes up most of the Earth. Its upper layer, about 300 kilometers (186 miles) thick, is able to move, like a very thick liquid. The heat flowing from the interior makes it churn—rather like the heat from a gas flame makes the soup in a pot rise and fall, except that the churning of the outer mantle takes millions of years.

HISTORY FILE

LIFE ON EARTH

Years ago (B=billions; M=millions)	
4.6B	Earth formed
3.8B	Simple life exists in the oceans
500M	First fish
400M	Plants appear on land
380M	Animals appear on land
350M	Reptiles develop
280M	Insects develop
225M	First mammals appear
200M	First birds
180M	Pangaea supercontinent breaks into two
65M	Extinction of dinosaurs and many other species
1.5M	Appearance of first human beings in East Africa

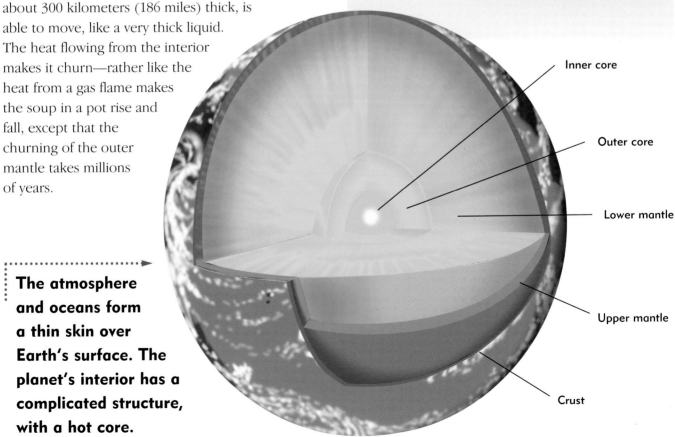

The atmosphere and oceans form a thin skin over Earth's surface. The planet's interior has a complicated structure, with a hot core.

Inner core

Outer core

Lower mantle

Upper mantle

Crust

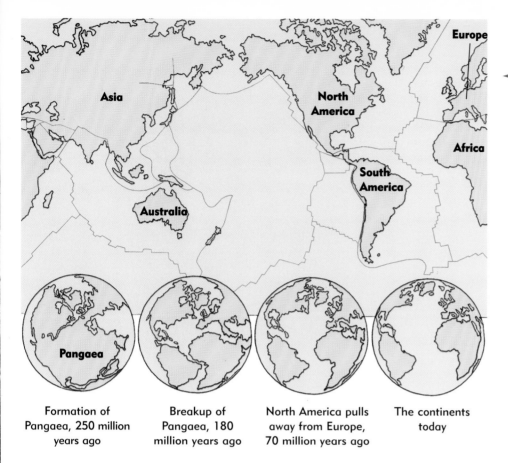

Asia

North America

Europe

Africa

South America

Australia

Pangaea

Formation of Pangaea, 250 million years ago

Breakup of Pangaea, 180 million years ago

North America pulls away from Europe, 70 million years ago

The continents today

The continents ride on rigid areas of the crust, called plates (the boundaries between the plates are shown in red). Today's continents were formed over the last 180 million years by the breakup of a single supercontinent called Pangaea.

Earth is the only planet that is rich in water and oxygen.

The Earth's Crust

The outermost layer of the Earth, the crust, consists of less dense rocks that float on the denser rock of the mantle. The crust is 5 to 10 kilometers (3 to 6 mi) thick beneath the oceans. The continents consist of crust 20 to 65 kilometers (12 to 40 mi) thick. Crustal rocks are mostly made of silicon and metals such as aluminum and iron, combined with oxygen. The rocks are moved around by the churning of the mantle rocks beneath. Over hundreds of millions of years, continents are carried around and collide with each other.

FACT FILE

EARTH DATA

Distance from Sun (mil. km/mi):	149.6/93
Year (Time to go round Sun):	365.26 days
Day (Time to revolve on axis):	23 hours, 56 mins
Diameter at Equator (km/mi):	12,756/7,926
Known moons:	1
Mass (Earth=1):	1 (= 6.6 sextillion)
Surface gravity (Earth=1):	1 (= 9.81 meters per second per second)

MARS

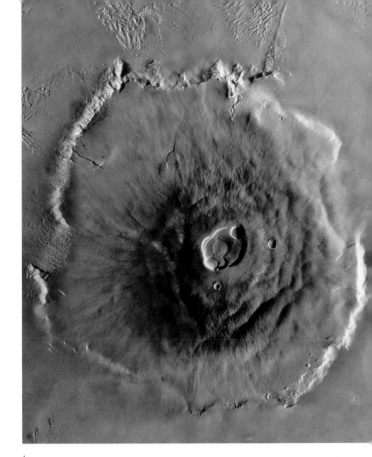

Mars is called the "red planet" because of its distinctive reddish coloring. It is red because its surface is a desert covered with sands made of compounds of iron and oxygen, similar to iron rust. The Martian atmosphere consists mostly of carbon dioxide. It is very thin, and its pressure at the surface is less than one-hundredth of that at Earth's surface. But winds on Mars are strong enough to raise sand storms that can hide the surface from view for weeks at a time.

The Ice Caps
The Martian atmosphere is so thin because gravity is too weak to hold an atmosphere. Liquid water cannot exist—it would soon turn into vapor. Most of the tiny amount of water on Mars is frozen in the polar caps. The southern cap is permanently coated with frozen carbon dioxide. The northern polar cap is coated with carbon dioxide during the winter, but this evaporates during the summer.

Giant Mons Olympus towers 27 kilometers (17 mi) above the Martian desert.

A huge system of canyons called Valles Marineris stretches for thousands of kilometers across Mars.

TEST FILE

WATCHING MARS
Mars is at its brightest roughly every 2 years and 7 weeks. It is then at opposition, that is, opposite to the Sun as seen from Earth. It rises in the east as the Sun is setting in the west and is high in the sky at midnight. These are the dates of opposition up to 2005, with the **constellations** where Mars can be found.

2001	June 13	Sagittarius
2003	August 28	Capricornus
2005	November 7	Aries

Millions of years ago Mars likely had a thicker atmosphere. There was liquid water on the surface, perhaps released when vast quantities of underground ice were melted by volcanic eruptions. Floods carved valleys that still exist today. A network of valleys, called the Valles Marineris, dwarfs the Grand Canyon on Earth. The system is 4,000 kilometers (2,486 mi) long—long enough to stretch across the United States—and is 700 kilometers (435 mi) across at its widest part and 7 kilometers (4.3 mi) deep.

Tall Mountains, Deep Valleys

Heat from inside Mars built up huge volcanoes in the past, though they are all inactive now. Mons Olympus is 27 kilometers (17 mi) high—the tallest mountain in the solar system. In the past, impacts with asteroids or comets have flung pieces of Martian rock into space, and some may have landed on Earth as **meteorites**. There are also thousands of craters on Mars, partly worn down by millions of years of sand storms.

Viking space probes that landed on Mars in 1976 searched for signs of life in rocks but found no definite evidence for it. Still, many scientists think there is a chance that simple forms of life exist near the polar caps or deep underground.

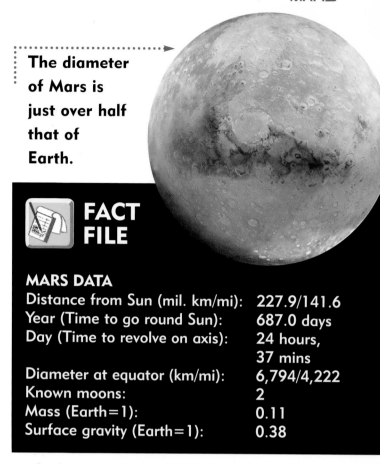

The diameter of Mars is just over half that of Earth.

FACT FILE

MARS DATA

Distance from Sun (mil. km/mi):	227.9/141.6
Year (Time to go round Sun):	687.0 days
Day (Time to revolve on axis):	24 hours, 37 mins
Diameter at equator (km/mi):	6,794/4,222
Known moons:	2
Mass (Earth=1):	0.11
Surface gravity (Earth=1):	0.38

Rocks are scattered over the Martian desert in this photograph taken by a Viking robot spacecraft that landed in 1976.

ASTEROIDS

Thousands of smaller bodies, called asteroids, planetoids, or minor planets, circle the Sun. Most move in orbits that lie between Mars and the next major planet, Jupiter. There is a large gap between these two planets, and in 1800 a group of astronomers got together to search for a faint planet moving in this region. They called themselves the "Celestial Police." But before they could start work, an Italian astronomer, Giuseppe Piazzi, found the first asteroid, later called Ceres. In the following six years, the Celestial Police found three more tiny asteroids—Pallas, Vesta, and Juno.

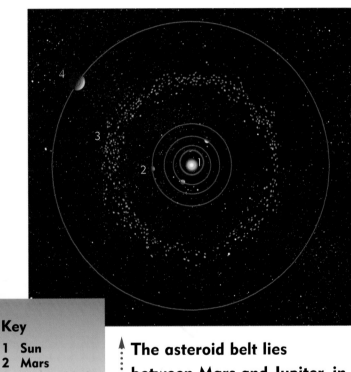

Key
1. Sun
2. Mars
3. Asteroid belt
4. Jupiter

The asteroid belt lies between Mars and Jupiter, in a gap in the planets' orbits.

Asteroids by the Thousand

The next asteroids were not found until 1845 and 1847. From then on not a year passed without more asteroids being discovered. From 1891, photography was used to search for asteroids, and then many were discovered. But of all the asteroids, only Vesta is ever bright enough to be seen with the naked eye.

Once it was thought that asteroids were the pieces of a planet that had been destroyed in an explosion or a collision. Now it is thought that they

TEST FILE

THE TITIUS–BODE RULE

The Celestial Police were guided in their search for asteroids by a rule named after two German astronomers, Johann Daniel Titius and Johann Elert Bode. The Titius–Bode rule generates a series of numbers in this way: Start with 0, 3, and then keep doubling the numbers after that, to give—
0, 3, 6, 12, 24, 48, 96, 192, 384, 768.

Add 4 to each number, to give—
4, 7, 10, 16, 28, 52, 100, 196, 388, 772.

Then divide by 10, to give—
0.4, 0.7, 1.0, 1.6, 2.8, 5.2, 10.0, 19.6, 38.8, 77.2.

Compare this series with the distances of the planets from the Sun (with the Earth–Sun distance taken as 1.0) as shown below.

Planet	True distance	Titius-Bode Rule distance
Mercury	0.4	0.4
Venus	0.7	0.7
Earth	1.0	1.0
Mars	1.5	1.6
		2.8
Jupiter	5.2	5.2
Saturn	9.5	10.0
Uranus	19.2	19.6
Neptune	30.1	38.8
Pluto	39.4	77.2

The numbers give a good approximation to the distances of the planets as far as Uranus (then the farthest known planet), except that there is a gap at 2.8. In this gap the astronomers discovered the asteroids.

consist of matter that was never able to gather into a single body because of the effect of Jupiter's gravity.

However, some of the asteroids have collided with each other and broken up in the past. One, Psyche, is almost pure nickel-iron—the same substance that the

The impact of an asteroid on Earth would almost certainly mean the death of the entire human race.

FUTURE FILE

WHAT IF AN ASTEROID HIT THE EARTH?
If an asteroid 1 kilometer (.6 mi) across hit Earth, it would blast a big area and create huge waves in the oceans and the ground itself. A dust cloud would be formed that would last for years, cooling the whole Earth. Humans would probably not survive. Many scientists believe that an impact like this—or the vast amounts of dust it would have caused—wiped out the dinosaurs and thousands of other animal and plant species 65 million years ago.

Moon. The asteroid was only about 10 meters (33 feet) across, but that would have been big enough to do considerable damage if it had hit Earth.

The asteroid Vesta is so small that its gravity is not strong enough to pull it into a rounded shape (see page 29).

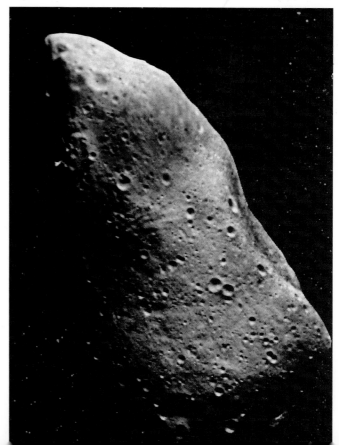

molten core of Earth is made of. Psyche was probably once part of the core of a larger body.

Small but Deadly

If all the asteroids, known and yet to be discovered, were put together, they would make only a tiny body, with a mass about one-thirtieth of the Moon's. The biggest, Ceres, accounts for nearly half the total mass of the asteroids.

Some asteroids move in orbits that take them far from the main belt between Mars and Jupiter. "Earth-crossing" asteroids are those whose orbits cross the orbit of Earth. Some come close to Earth by astronomical standards. In 1994 an asteroid called XM_1 passed within 104,000 kilometers (64,624 mi) of Earth. That is about one-fourth of the distance to the

JUPITER

The giant planet Jupiter is as large as 1,500 Earths. The planet consists of a great ball of hydrogen and helium, with small amounts of other elements—a sample of the gases from which the whole solar system formed. We are able to see only the tops of the clouds of frozen ammonia crystals that cover the planet. The clouds form dark-colored stripes called belts, and light ones called zones.

In the southern hemisphere is the Great Red Spot, a swirling storm that is broader than Earth. The Great Red Spot was first observed in 1664 or 1665, when telescopes first became powerful enough to reveal it, and it shows no signs of dying away. There are smaller storms over the whole planet, and lightning flashes send out radio noise that can be detected on Earth.

Jupiter, the largest planet in the solar system, is a globe of hydrogen, helium, and other gases over 1,500 times the size of Earth.

TEST FILE

WATCHING JUPITER
Jupiter is at its brightest when it is opposite in the sky to the Sun. It is then high in the sky at midnight. At its brightest, Jupiter appears brighter than any other planet except Venus. Here the dates of opposition up to 2005 are given, along with the constellations in which Jupiter is found.

2000	November 28	Taurus
2001	(not at opposition)	
2002	January 1	Gemini
2003	February 2	Cancer
2004	March 4	Leo
2005	April 3	Virgo

The Structure of Jupiter
The gaseous part of Jupiter's atmosphere probably takes up the top 1,000 kilometers (620 mi) of the planet. The pressure below this layer is enormous, crushing the hydrogen gas into liquid form. Deeper down, the hydrogen is compressed into a hard, metal-like form. At the very center of Jupiter, there is probably a core of rock and iron. Jupiter gives out more heat than it receives from the Sun, and its center is believed to be at least 20,000°C (36,032°F) —far hotter than the surface of the Sun.

FACT FILE

JUPITER DATA

Distance from Sun (mil. km/mi):	778/484
Year (Time to go round Sun):	11.9 years
Day (Time to revolve on axis):	9 hours, 50 mins
Diameter at equator (km/mi):	142,984/ 88,850
Known moons:	16
Mass (Earth=1):	317.8
Surface gravity (Earth=1):	2.4

The Great Red Spot is a storm in Jupiter's atmosphere that has been raging for centuries.

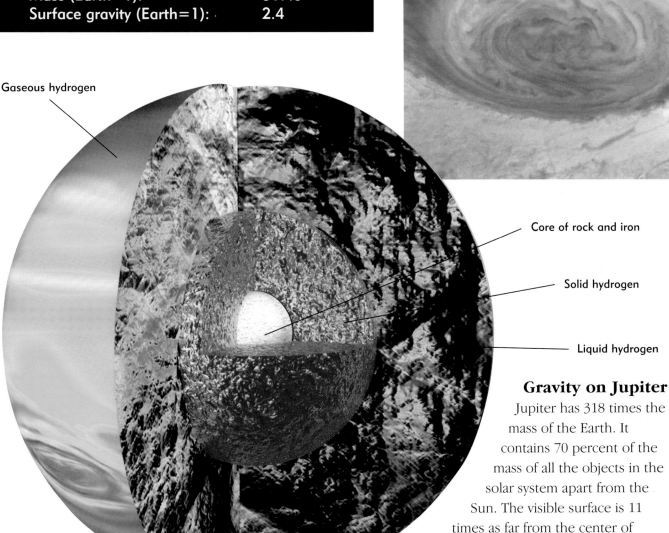

Gaseous hydrogen

Core of rock and iron

Solid hydrogen

Liquid hydrogen

Inside Jupiter the tremendous pressure crushes the hydrogen gas into liquid and solid forms. There may be a small core of rock and iron.

Gravity on Jupiter

Jupiter has 318 times the mass of the Earth. It contains 70 percent of the mass of all the objects in the solar system apart from the Sun. The visible surface is 11 times as far from the center of Jupiter as Earth's surface is from our planet's center. So despite the planet's huge mass, the force of gravity at the surface is only 2.4 times that on Earth. Jupiter rotates in less than 10 hours—so fast that the atmosphere is thrown outward strongly at the equator. Through a telescope, the planet can clearly be seen to be elliptical.

SATURN

Among the planets Saturn is second only to Jupiter in size. Its orbit is 9.5 times farther from the Sun than Earth's is. It is cold and dark this far from the Sun: Saturn receives less than one ninetieth as much light and heat as Earth. But the planet is girdled by spectacular broad, flat rings, more impressive than any others in the solar system.

Saturn's Rings

The rings are made of millions of small chunks of matter, each following its own orbit around the planet. The chunks are made of ordinary ice or of rock coated with ice. No one knows whether the rings were formed at the same time as Saturn, or were produced later by the collision of two small satellites or asteroids.

Through Earth-based telescopes, the rings look flat and featureless, apart from several gaps. But the *Voyager 1* spacecraft, which visited Saturn in 1980, discovered that they are made up of at least 10,000 thin individual rings called ringlets.

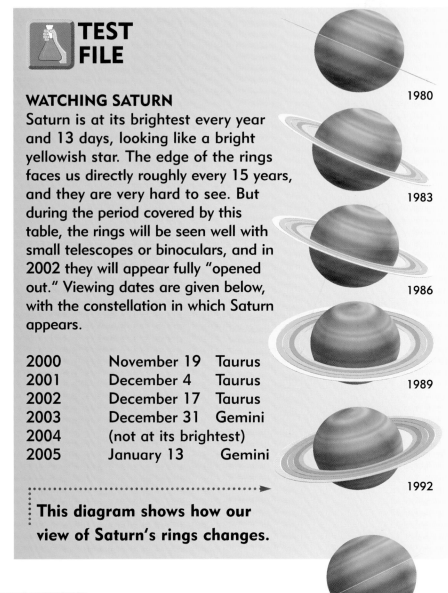

TEST FILE

WATCHING SATURN
Saturn is at its brightest every year and 13 days, looking like a bright yellowish star. The edge of the rings faces us directly roughly every 15 years, and they are very hard to see. But during the period covered by this table, the rings will be seen well with small telescopes or binoculars, and in 2002 they will appear fully "opened out." Viewing dates are given below, with the constellation in which Saturn appears.

Year	Date	Constellation
2000	November 19	Taurus
2001	December 4	Taurus
2002	December 17	Taurus
2003	December 31	Gemini
2004	(not at its brightest)	
2005	January 13	Gemini

This diagram shows how our view of Saturn's rings changes.

1980
1983
1986
1989
1992
1995

Some of the thousands of ringlets that make up the rings of Saturn. This picture was taken by the *Voyager 2* spacecraft.

Some gaps in the rings are caused by the gravity of Saturn's inner satellites. The tiny satellite Pan actually moves inside a gap called Encke's Division. The most sharply defined gap, called Cassini's Division, is caused by Mimas and Enceladus, which lie well beyond the rings. Other satellites affect the ringlets, giving some of them a kinked or braided appearance.

FACT FILE

SATURN DATA

Distance from Sun (mil. km/mi):	1,427/887
Year (Time to go round Sun):	29.5 years
Day (Time to revolve on axis):	10 hours, 14 mins
Diameter at equator (km/mi):	120,536/ 74,901
Known moons:	18
Mass (Earth=1):	95.1
Surface gravity (Earth=1):	1.15

The Composition of Saturn

Like Jupiter, Saturn is made up mostly of hydrogen, with some helium and traces of other gases. At the center there is likely a solid, rocky core, at a temperature of at least 15,000°C (27,000°F). Outside this the hydrogen is crushed into a hard, metal-like state by the pressure. Above this, from about the halfway point, the hydrogen is liquid. Outside this liquid layer is the gaseous hydrogen atmosphere. The cloud tops are not as strongly marked as those on Jupiter, but brown and white spots and cloud belts have been observed by spacecraft and Earth-based telescopes.

The shape of Saturn is flattened at the top and bottom.

1997

2000

2003

2006

2009

FUTURE FILE

THE CASSINI MISSION

In October 1997 the *Cassini* spacecraft was launched from Cape Canaveral on a 7-year journey to Saturn. The survey of Saturn and its moons following its arrival in July 2004 is designed to last at least 4 years. *Cassini* carried a probe called *Huygens*, designed to parachute onto Saturn's moon Titan and make observations of its surface and atmosphere.

URANUS AND NEPTUNE

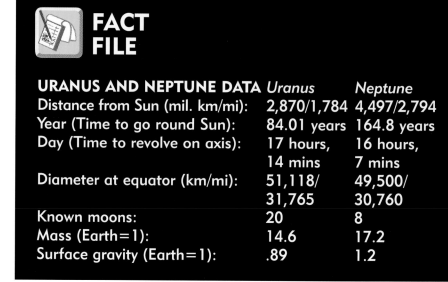

FACT FILE

URANUS AND NEPTUNE DATA	*Uranus*	*Neptune*
Distance from Sun (mil. km/mi):	2,870/1,784	4,497/2,794
Year (Time to go round Sun):	84.01 years	164.8 years
Day (Time to revolve on axis):	17 hours,	16 hours,
	14 mins	7 mins
Diameter at equator (km/mi):	51,118/	49,500/
	31,765	30,760
Known moons:	20	8
Mass (Earth=1):	14.6	17.2
Surface gravity (Earth=1):	.89	1.2

ar beyond Saturn, the third of the gas giants, Uranus, moves around the Sun. It takes more than 84 Earth years to complete one orbit. Uranus is just visible to the naked eye as a dim "star," at present in the constellation Capricornus. In 1781 the astronomer William Herschel looked at it through a telescope and saw a small disc instead of a point of light. He thought at first it was a comet, but its motion showed it was a planet, the first new planet to be discovered beyond Saturn.

Key

1 Uranus
2 Miranda
3 Ariel
4 Umbriel
5 Titania
6 Oberon

← Orbit of Uranus around the Sun

The moons of Uranus revolve almost at right angles to the direction of the planet's orbit around the Sun.

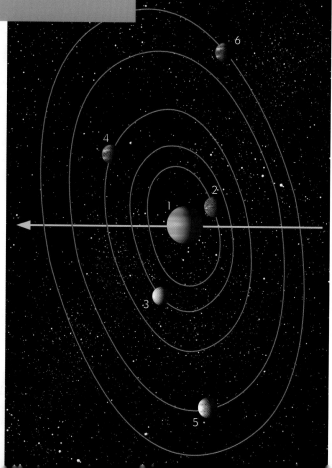

Rolling Around the Sun

Uranus seems to lie on its side—the axis around which it spins is tilted over more than 90°. This means that each pole is in sunlight for half of the planet's year, while the other pole is in darkness.

Uranus is bluish-green with hardly any visible markings. Though it is smaller than Jupiter and Saturn, Uranus is still 64 times larger than Earth. It is mostly made up of hydrogen and helium, but its color is due to methane crystals in its atmosphere. Beneath the outer gaseous atmosphere is a mantle containing ammonia and frozen water. At the center of the planet there may be a rocky core.

The Blue Planet

Neptune is almost exactly the same size as Uranus, but it is bluer in color. It is about 30 times as far from the Sun as Earth is and takes just under 165 Earth years to go around the Sun. Not until the year 2011 will it have completed one orbit of the Sun since its discovery in September 1846. Neptune gets little more than a thousandth of the light and heat that we get from the Sun.

But Neptune is no colder than Uranus because more heat flows from its interior. This flow of heat churns up the atmosphere and makes weather on Neptune more dynamic than it is on Uranus. Strong winds blow around the planet. When the *Voyager 2* spacecraft flew past Neptune in 1989, it spotted an area

A bright white cloud of methane crystals appears near the top of this false-color image of Uranus.

High-altitude clouds float above the bluish methane haze of Neptune.

of storms called the Great Dark Spot south of the equator. The area is larger across than the diameter of Earth. Elsewhere on the planet, other storms were going on. They included a disturbance topped by bright clouds, called the Scooter.

HISTORY FILE

NEPTUNE—THE PLANET FOUND ON PAPER

After its discovery in 1781, astronomers noticed that the speed at which Uranus orbits is irregular. Several astronomers had the idea that its movement was being disturbed by the gravitational pull of an unknown planet beyond it. Two young mathematicians, the Englishman John Couch Adams and the Frenchman Urbain Leverrier, not knowing of each other's work, calculated where such a planet must be and its approximate mass. Their results were very similar, but it was using Leverrier's results that German astronomers found the new planet close to the position he had predicted. This was a triumph for the theory of gravitation, which was shown to work for the farthest planets.

PLUTO AND BEYOND

Beyond Neptune the solar system is fringed by a belt of small, rocky objects. The largest of these, the planet Pluto, was discovered in 1930, and others began to be discovered in 1992. Astronomers believe there may be thousands of them.

HISTORY FILE

THE WRONG PLANET IN THE RIGHT PLACE

Even after the discovery of Neptune, astronomers thought there were disturbances of Uranus that Neptune couldn't be responsible for. The astronomer Percival Lowell worked out the probable size, mass, and orbit of a new planet, and spent years searching for it. In 1929, 13 years after Lowell's death, Clyde Tombaugh took up the search and found Pluto in January 1930. Its position and orbit were close to what Lowell had predicted, but Pluto is far too small to have affected Uranus noticeably. Besides, there do not now seem to be any disturbances to the orbit of Uranus apart from those due to Neptune. Finding Pluto appears to have been a fluke.

Pluto is usually regarded as the outermost planet, but perhaps it should not be counted as a planet at all. It is smaller than some of the moons of the gas giants. It is likely made of a mixture of rock and ice as most of the moons are. And it follows a strange orbit, sharply tilted compared to the orbits of the other planets, and strongly elliptical. At its farthest point, it is 49 times as far from the Sun as Earth is. But at its closest, it comes closer to the Sun than Neptune does, though because of the tilt of its orbit, it is never close enough to Neptune to collide with it.

The Double Planet

Pluto is so tiny and distant that detail on its surface cannot be made out by Earth-based telescopes. But Pluto has a satellite, Charon, whose diameter is 55 percent of the diameter of Pluto, making the pair more like a double planet than an ordinary planet and satellite. Charon was discovered in 1978. Then astronomers had a piece of luck: From 1985 to 1990 Charon happened to pass repeatedly between Earth and Pluto, something that won't happen again for 120 years. By studying the way the brightness of Pluto changed as Charon passed, astronomers could roughly map light and dark areas on Pluto's surface. They have also discovered that frozen methane and nitrogen cover its surface.

The distant Sun feebly lights up the dark, frozen surface of Pluto.

Pluto and Charon make a double planet that should perhaps be regarded as the largest of the Kuiper Belt Objects.

The Kuiper Belt

For a long time, astronomers have searched for objects beyond Pluto. If there are any large objects, they are too far away to affect the known planets noticeably by their gravity. But around 1950 two astronomers, Kenneth Essex Edgeworth and Gerard Kuiper, independently suggested that some comets come from a belt of unseen objects circling the Sun at about the distance of Pluto, or farther. The first object in what is now called the Kuiper Belt was found in 1992. Within a few years, 60 of these KBOs (Kuiper Belt Objects) had been discovered. The largest was only 500 kilometers (311 mi) across. Objects as small as this, or smaller, do not have strong enough gravity

to be pulled into a round shape. About half of all known KBOs are trapped by Neptune's gravity, moving around the Sun in 1.5 times as long as it takes Neptune. Pluto moves in the same way, so these KBOs are called "Plutinos" (little Plutos).

The KBOs are matter "left over" from the birth of the solar system. If all of them (including the still undiscovered ones) were put together, they would probably make a single planet about the size of Earth. Some astronomers hope to find a "Planet X," at least as large as Pluto, out beyond the known planets. This is still possible. But such a planet would have to be very faint and slow-moving to have been missed, and very far away indeed.

PLANETARY MOONS

There are few natural satellites in the inner solar system. Mercury and Venus have none. Earth has just one, the Moon. Mars has two tiny satellites, which are probably asteroids that were captured by the planet's gravity.

But things are very different in the outer solar system. The four gas giants are surrounded by their own small systems of orbiting moons. Jupiter has 16 satellites, Saturn 18, Uranus 20, and Neptune 8.

Birth of the Satellites

Jupiter's moons demonstrate how planets came to have satellites. The eight innermost moons were created at the same time as the planet. They orbit above Jupiter's equator and move in the same direction that Jupiter rotates.

The next four satellites form a group, with a big gap between them and the inner moons. Their orbits are strongly tilted in relation to Jupiter's equator. Far beyond these is another group of four, also strongly tilted and revolving around the planet in the opposite direction to all the rest. These two groups were probably formed from asteroids being broken up by impacts and captured by Jupiter's gravity.

Fire and Ice

Satellites can be very different from each other. Io, the innermost of the four largest moons of Jupiter, is highly volcanic. Its interior is heated as Io is stretched and squeezed by Jupiter's gravitational field, and the result is continuous spectacular volcanic eruptions of orange, white, and black sulfur. These volcanoes are the hottest surface locations anywhere in the solar system apart from the Sun.

Another satellite of Jupiter, Europa, is covered

Europa

Triton

Io

Ganymede

our Moon

Callisto

Titan

The largest moons in the solar system are larger than the planet Pluto.

The nine largest satellites of Saturn. Phoebe and Iapetus are so far away from Saturn that they have to be shown separately.

Key

1 Saturn
2 Mimas
3 Enceladus
4 Tethys
5 Dione
6 Rhea
7 Titan
8 Hyperion
9 Iapetus
10 Phoebe

with a smooth layer of ice, perhaps 100 kilometers (62 mi) thick. The satellite looks as smooth as a billiard ball. Beneath the ice there is probably water, and it is possible that primitive life has developed there. Callisto—another of Jupiter's satellites—is also covered with ice but the surface is cratered and rough. Scientists believe there is salty water under the ice.

Saturn's largest moon, Titan, has a thick atmosphere, composed mostly of nitrogen. Early in the twenty-first century the *Huygens* space probe will parachute into Titan's atmosphere to study this moon and see whether conditions exist similar to those on Earth before life appeared—or even whether simple life has developed.

The most battered-looking satellite in the solar system is Miranda, a small moon of Uranus. The surface of Miranda is torn by huge valleys and ridges. Miranda seems to have been smashed by some impact in the past, with the pieces reassembling themselves afterward.

A sulfur volcano erupts on the horizon of Io, the volcanic satellite of Jupiter. Reddish sulfur compounds produced in past eruptions cover the surface.

FUTURE FILE

THE FATE OF THE MOONS
All satellites' orbits change over time. Our Moon is slowly spiraling away from Earth. But Triton, the largest moon of Neptune, is slowly spiraling inward towards the planet. In a billion years, Triton will probably break up to form a ring more spectacular than Saturn's.

METEORS AND METEORITES

Watch the sky on a clear night, and several times in an hour you will see what seems to be a star darting across the night sky and disappearing. Sometimes it leaves a trail that glows briefly. This "shooting star" or "falling star" is caused by particles of matter falling to Earth from space and burning up because of friction with the air. The scientific name for a shooting star is a **meteor** and the clump of matter that causes it is called a **meteoroid**.

FACT FILE

METEOR AND METEORITE DATA

★ Largest meteorite: fell in prehistoric times at Hoba West, near Grootfontein, Namibia; weight: 65 tons (meteorite still lies where it fell).

★ Heaviest meteor shower of modern times: the Leonid of 1966, which on November 17 reached a rate of 60,000 per hour for 40 minutes.

★ Best-preserved meteorite crater: Meteor Crater (also called Barringer Crater) in Arizona; 1.26 kilometers (.8 mi) wide, 175 meters (574 ft) deep.

★ Mass of meteoroids entering atmosphere daily: approximately 1,100 tons.

★ Average speed of observed meteors: 40 kilometers (25 mi) per second.

Pieces of rock are mixed with iron in this thin slice of a meteorite found in the Chilean desert.

Meteor Crater in Arizona was probably formed about 27,000 years ago.

Comet Dust

Meteor showers can be seen on certain dates every year. The number of meteors can briefly rise to hundreds or even thousands per hour at these times. Meteor showers occur when Earth crosses a trail of dust left behind by a comet along its orbit—either a comet that still exists or one that has broken up. For example, two showers called the Eta Aquarids and the Orionids are seen once a year on the separate occasions when Earth crosses the dust trail of Halley's comet.

Very occasionally, larger chunks of rock, so big that they are not completely burned away, enter the atmosphere. The remaining piece of rock that falls to the ground is called a **meteorite**. People have been slightly injured by meteorites, but no one is known to have been killed by one.

Meteorites seem to have come from asteroids that have been broken up by collisions. Most are stony, but some are metallic, made of iron and nickel.

Meteorites from Mars

Some meteorites seem, from the minerals they are made of, to have come from Mars. They may have been blown off the planet either by huge volcanic eruptions or by the impact of asteroids or large meteorites on Mars. In 1997 there was excitement when scientists claimed to have found substances in such meteorites produced by simple life forms. But many scientists now think the substances were formed on Earth in other ways.

A glowing meteor trail is left as a grain of interplanetary dust hurtles through the atmosphere and is burned up by friction.

TEST FILE

MAJOR METEOR SHOWERS

A meteor shower builds up to a maximum over several days or even weeks and then dies away again. Meteors can appear all over the sky, but if their paths are traced back, they seem to come from a single point, called the radiant of the shower. The shower is named after the constellation in which the radiant lies. Meteor showers appear on the same dates each year.

Date of Maximum	Name of Shower	Position of Radiant
January 3	Quadrantids	Boötes (there used to be a constellation here called The Quadrant)
May 4	Eta Aquarids	Aquarius (near star Eta Aquarii)
August 11	Perseids	Perseus
October 20	Orionids	Orion
November 16	Leonids	Leo
December 13	Geminids	Gemini

COMETS

Every few years a spectacular comet crosses the skies. It starts far from the Sun, a faint dot of light looking like a fuzzy star. But over a period of months, as it comes closer to the Sun, it grows a tail, or, more usually, two—one a misty, curved tail of dust, the other a straight tail of glowing gas. At its closest to the Sun, the comet may have tails stretching across millions of kilometers of space. As the comet moves away from the Sun, its tails shorten and grow fainter, and finally disappear.

Most comets are seen only once. But some reappear, again and again, moving around elliptical orbits. Halley's comet, the most famous comet of all, travels as close as 90 million kilometers to the Sun— 60 percent of the Earth's distance. In the outermost part of its orbit, the comet travels out to 35 times Earth's distance from the Sun—beyond the orbit of Neptune.

Gas and dust stream from the nucleus of Halley's comet, as photographed by the *Giotto* spacecraft.

Some comets take much longer to revisit the inner solar system. One of the most spectacular comets of recent years was Hale-Bopp, which passed the Sun on April 1, 1998. By studying its movements, astronomers calculated that it had last passed Earth in 2214 B.C. If it isn't disturbed by some object in the outer solar system, it will return in the year 6210.

A comet's tail always points away from the Sun. It grows as it approaches the Sun and shrinks as it moves away.

FACT FILE

WHEN HALLEY MET GIOTTO

Space probes from several nations flew close to Halley's comet at its most recent appearance in 1986. The European Space Agency craft *Giotto* came closest. Some of its instruments were knocked out as the probe was blasted by a dust storm from the comet. Pictures from *Giotto* showed the nucleus was darker than coal.

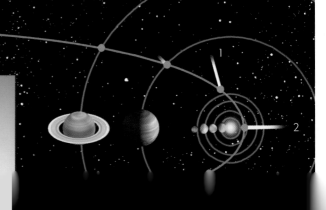

Key
1. Tail lengthens as comet approaches Sun
2. Tail longest closest to Sun
3. Tail shrinks as comet moves away from Sun
→ Path of comet

HISTORY FILE

NOTABLE COMETS

★ Comets have collided with Earth in the past. One may have caused the devastation of an area of forest 600 kilometers (373 mi) across in the Tunguska region of Siberia in 1908. Fortunately the area was uninhabited.

★ Comet Encke has been seen scores of times, because it takes slightly less than 3 years and 4 months to go round the Sun. It comes closer to the Sun than Mercury's average distance.

★ People used to think that every comet was a completely new event. The seventeenth-century English astronomer Edmond Halley realized that a certain comet was reappearing about every 76 years. Halley predicted that it would come again in 1758. It appeared on time, and was named after him.

★ The Great Comet of 1843 developed a tail that was 330 million kilometers (205 million mi) long—more than twice the distance of Earth from the Sun.

★ In 1910 there were prophecies that all life on Earth would be wiped out when Earth passed through the tail of Halley's comet. In fact, the event had no effect on Earth at all.

★ In June 1998 the *SOHO (Solar and Heliospheric Observatory)* robot space probe observed two comets crashing into the Sun. The tiny mass of the comets made no noticeable impact on the Sun.

Anatomy of a Comet

The solid part of a comet is called the nucleus. The nucleus is a mixture of rock and "ices." Ices are not just frozen water but can be frozen carbon dioxide, methane, or ammonia. There are two vast stores of millions of comet nuclei beyond the planets. One is the Kuiper Belt, just outside the orbit of Neptune; the other is the Oort Cloud, which forms a spherical shell around the solar system. From time to time, one of these "sleeping comets" starts to fall inward towards the Sun.

When a comet nucleus comes within the distance of Jupiter's orbit from the Sun, the warmth of the Sun causes some of the ice to turn into gas. Great fountains of gas and dust erupt from the nucleus. The gas spreads out around the nucleus in a huge globe, called the coma. The solar wind, a constant stream of subatomic particles (mostly protons and electrons) from the Sun, blows the gas and dust away from the comet nucleus to form the tails.

Halley's comet reappears about every 76 years and usually makes a spectacular sight.

EXPLORATION

Human beings have taken just a few small steps on the long journey of exploring the solar system. The first journey beyond Earth was a single orbit of the planet by the Russian cosmonaut Yuri Gagarin in 1961. In 1969 the first American astronauts traveled to the Moon. In six missions over the next 3½ years, 12 men walked on the Moon, studied its rocks, and brought samples back to Earth.

Crowded Orbits

Though human beings have not been back to the Moon since 1972, many have gone into orbit around Earth. Only Russia and the United States launch manned spacecraft, but they carry space travelers of many nationalities.

The neighborhood of Earth has become more and more crowded. Thousands of satellites have been launched to survey the weather and climate; carry TV, radio, and phone signals and computer data; spy on military secrets; study the planet's resources; and view space from above our hazy, turbulent atmosphere.

A Voyager space probe flying past Saturn

This multiple-exposure picture shows a U.S. Titan II rocket being raised into launch position and lifting off carrying a Gemini two-person capsule.

Robot Explorers

Unmanned space probes have led the way across the solar system. They orbited the Moon and made crash landings before the first landing by astronauts. The first craft to fly by another planet was the American *Mariner 2* in 1962, flying past Venus. Later, Soviet probes parachuted down through the atmosphere of Venus and sent back photographs of the surface before the heat and pressure destroyed them.

In 1976 two American Viking craft landed on Mars, sent back pictures of the surface, and carried out chemical experiments to search for life in the soil. In 1997 they were followed by the *Pathfinder* mission, which carried a small robot rover.

Space Odysseys

In the 1970s two Pioneer spacecraft and two Voyager craft were launched and carried out some of the greatest space journeys ever. Visiting Jupiter first, they used its huge gravity field to propel them on, gaining a speed boost that carried them on past the other outer planets. Between them the craft visited the vicinities of Saturn, Uranus, and Neptune, leaving Pluto the only planet in the solar system that has not yet been visited. Now they will drift away from the region of the planets, until in hundreds of thousands of years they may reach other planetary systems.

FACT FILE

MILESTONES IN SPACE EXPLORATION

This table shows some important space missions. They are not necessarily the first of their kind, but they are the first really successful ones.

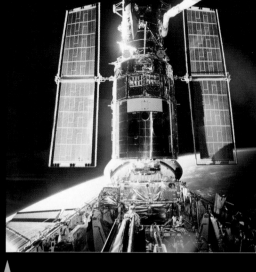

The Hubble Space Telescope is launched from space shuttle *Discovery* April 25, 1990.

Launch date	Craft	Mission Notes
April 12, 1961	Vostok 1	Yuri Gagarin, first human being in space, orbited Earth.
August 27, 1962	Mariner 2	Flyby of Venus.
July 16, 1969	Apollo 11	First Moon landing.
August 17, 1970	Venera 7	Venus landing—transmitted for 23 minutes after landing.
March 2,1972	Pioneer 10	Flew past Jupiter; followed a year later by *Pioneer 11*, which also flew by Saturn.
November 3, 1973	Mariner 10	First probe to observe Mercury, following Venus flyby.
August 20, 1975	Viking 1	Mission to Mars with orbiter and lander; closely followed by *Viking 2*. Both landers transmitted data for years.
September 5, 1977	Voyager 1	Flew by Jupiter and Saturn. *Voyager 2* followed and visited Jupiter, Saturn, Uranus, and Neptune.
April 12, 1981	Space Shuttle	First flight of reusable spacecraft to Earth orbit .
July 2, 1985	Giotto	Close approach to nucleus of Halley's comet. Japanese and Russian spacecraft also observed the comet.
February 20, 1986	Mir	Soviet (now Russian) space station. Cosmonauts have set endurance records, some staying in space for over a year.
October 18, 1989	Galileo	Probe parachuted into Jupiter's atmosphere; orbiter reported on Jupiter's satellites.
October 6, 1990	Ulysses	Flew by Jupiter and went on to fly over poles of Sun.
December 4, 1996	Pathfinder	Explored a small area of Mars with *Sojourner*, a mini-rover vehicle.
October 15, 1997	Cassini	Probe to Saturn, due to arrive in 2004 and parachute *Huygens* probe into atmosphere of satellite Titan.

The *Huygens* probe will parachute down through the smoggy atmosphere of Titan, Saturn's largest moon.

MOON LANDINGS

Between 1969 and 1972, human beings explored a few small regions of the Moon. This U.S. Moon program, called Apollo, can be seen as a dress rehearsal for establishing settlements on the Moon and for journeys to the planets beyond.

Soviet robot crafts led the way: *Luna 2* crashed on the Moon in 1959 and *Luna 9* made the first soft landing in 1966. Then human beings followed. *Apollo 8* was a 1968 test flight on which a crew of three flew around the Moon and back to Earth. In May 1969 *Apollo 10* went into orbit around the Moon. This time the lunar module—the part of the spacecraft designed to land on the Moon—separated from the command module. It descended to within 15 kilometers (9 mi) of the surface before rejoining the command module for the journey home.

The Giant Leap

On July 16, 1969, *Apollo 11* took off on its way to the Moon, commanded by Neil Armstrong. On July 20 the lunar module *Eagle* touched down on a vast, rocky plain called the Sea of Tranquility. Watched by the world on TV, Armstrong crawled out of the lunar module and spoke his famous line: "That's one small step for a man, one giant leap for mankind." He was followed by the lunar module pilot, Edwin "Buzz" Aldrin. They gathered rocks and soil, set up several experiments, and raised an American flag. Then they blasted off, rejoined the command module, which was orbiting the Moon, piloted by Michael Collins, and returned to Earth.

> The sequence of maneuvers that took the Apollo astronauts to the Moon and back. To simplify the diagram, the Moon is shown in three positions along its orbit around Earth.

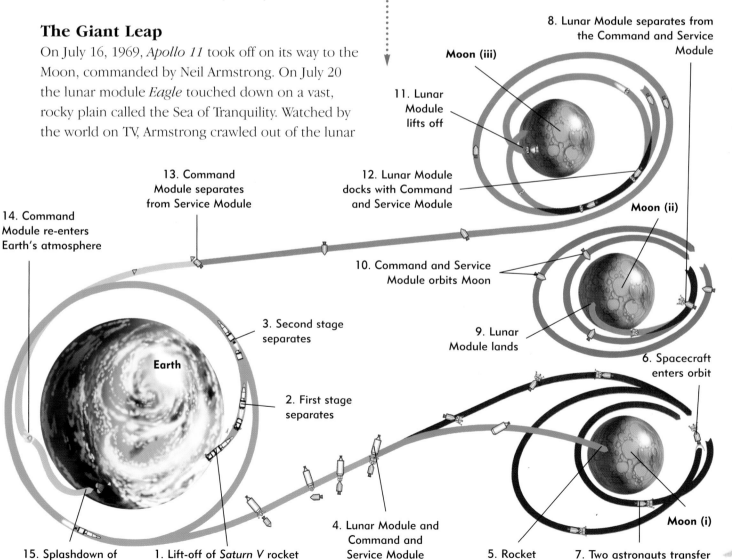

8. Lunar Module separates from the Command and Service Module

Moon (iii)

11. Lunar Module lifts off

13. Command Module separates from Service Module

12. Lunar Module docks with Command and Service Module

Moon (ii)

14. Command Module re-enters Earth's atmosphere

10. Command and Service Module orbits Moon

9. Lunar Module lands

6. Spacecraft enters orbit

3. Second stage separates

Earth

2. First stage separates

Moon (i)

15. Splashdown of Command Module

1. Lift-off of *Saturn V* rocket with Apollo spacecraft

4. Lunar Module and Command and Service Module separate from rocket

5. Rocket crashes on Moon

7. Two astronauts transfer to Lunar Module

APOLLO MISSION DATA
(Mission/Landing date/Landing site/
Mission notes)

★ *Apollo 11*
July 20, 1969
Sea of Tranquillity
First landing on the Moon by humans.

★ *Apollo 12*
November 19, 1969
Ocean of Storms
Landed near *Surveyor 3*, which had
landed 2 years before.

★ *Apollo 13*
(no landing)
Oxygen tank exploded and power was
reduced. Craft rounded Moon and
returned, and crew were saved.

★ *Apollo 14*
February 5, 1971
Crater Fra Mauro
Astronauts used a handcart to carry
equipment and rock samples.

★ *Apollo 15*
July 30, 1971
Hadley Rille
First use of a lunar rover vehicle.

★ *Apollo 16*
April 20, 1972
Region near crater Descartes
Mission commander carried out speed
and turning trials of the lunar rover.

★ *Apollo 17*
December 11, 1972
Near crater Littrow in Taurus mountains
Longest Apollo mission, and the last.

**An *Apollo 15* astronaut on the Moon.
On the right of the picture is the
lunar rover.**

The landing sites of the Apollo missions

Later Missions

There were six more Apollo launches. *Apollo 13* was
a near-disaster when an onboard explosion occurred.
The crippled craft could not land on the Moon, but it
had to fly around it before returning to Earth and
splashing down safely in the Pacific Ocean.

The other missions were completely successful.
But there have been no more visitors to the surface
of the Moon since Eugene Cernan, commander of
the *Apollo 17* mission, climbed into his lunar module
in December 1972 and returned to Earth.

The International Space Station, the first colony in space, began to be assembled in orbit in November 1998.

The DC-XA is a planned U.S. reusable spacecraft, designed to be lighter and cheaper than the space shuttle.

We are still busily exploring the solar system, and robot probes are leading the way. The *Galileo* spacecraft, which arrived at Jupiter in 1995, is still wandering among the giant planet's satellites. The *Cassini/Huygens* expedition will vastly increase our knowledge of Saturn and its satellites during the mission planned to begin in 2004, when it arrives at the planet. The *Pluto Kuiper Express* is expected to fly by Pluto, the last unvisited planet, in about 2011. Someday robot explorers may work successfully in the extreme heat and pressure on the surface of Venus.

The twenty-first century will see new telescopes in space. Giant radio observatories may be built on the far side of the Moon, where they will be shielded from the radio pollution of the Earth. The Next Generation Space Telescope—a more advanced version of today's Hubble Space Telescope—is planned to observe infrared rays, or heat radiation, from the universe. It will be placed in an orbit somewhere beyond the Moon, so that it is not affected by the heat that radiates from Earth.

In this artist's impression, the first explorers on Mars observe a sandstorm.

Colonizing Space

As the twenty-first century progresses, human beings may spread through the solar system. The International Space Station, in orbit around Earth, will probably grow larger. Space tourism might develop, with fare-paying travelers spending weekends in orbit and taking vacations on the Moon.

Huge space colonies may be built in orbit around Earth. They will probably be built in the form of rotating wheels. People inside the rim of the wheel will be pressed toward the outside, feeling a simulated force of gravity. This should avoid the problems of the weakening of bones and muscles that are caused by prolonged weightlessness.

The Search For Life

Missions lasting many years may travel to Mars and then to the outer solar system. If they do, they will look for clues to the formation of the planets and the solar system in general. And they will search for traces of primitive life. Promising places to look are in liquid water beneath the ice that covers the surfaces of some satellites or floats in the atmospheres of the giant planets.

 FUTURE FILE

CROSSING THE SOLAR SYSTEM

Present-day journeys to the outer solar system take years. New types of propulsion are needed for spacecraft. A slow, steady thrust continued for months or years could build up a large final speed. One possibility is nuclear energy; another is the "light-yacht," which would have large sails and would be pushed along by the pressure of sunlight. A stronger thrust could be provided by atoms of **antimatter**, which are "mirror-image" versions of ordinary atoms. When matter and antimatter collide, both vanish with the release of huge amounts of energy. If large amounts of antimatter could be made and safely stored, it could drive a spacecraft across the solar system at high speeds.

DEATH OF THE SOLAR SYSTEM

For as long as the Sun lasts, the planets will circle it steadily, disturbed only by the occasional asteroid or comet impact. But far in the future, the solar system will die. The Sun has been shining for about 5 billion years, and there have been changes in its brightness during that time. It may become hotter during the next billion years, making life impossible on Earth.

But even if the Sun doesn't change during this time, it will run low on hydrogen in another 5 billion years and will begin to burn helium instead. The change will prolong its life but will certainly spell the end of life on Earth. The aging Sun will swell to become a red giant star. It will become more than a hundred times as wide, swallowing Mercury and Venus and filling the present orbit of Earth.

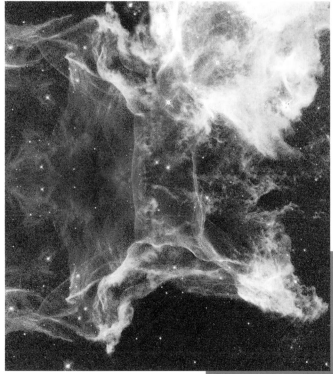

 **FUTURE FILE**

THE END OF THE UNIVERSE
Astronomers think that long after the Sun has faded into darkness, other stars will be born from the gas clouds scattered through the Galaxy. But eventually the gas will be used up and starbirth will cease after a trillion years. Yet the smallest, faintest stars may shine for 100 times longer than this. Much later, some of the dead stars will be swallowed into **black holes** growing at the heart of each galaxy, but most will escape from their galaxies and wander through space. The universe will have become a cold, dark place. No one knows whether life will evolve into a form that can survive into this distant future.

These interstellar gas clouds have been disturbed by the shock wave from a supernova—a star that has exploded.

About 5 billion years from now, Earth may be roasted by the swollen, dying Sun.

Roasting the Earth

The Earth's orbit will expand as the Sun loses mass. Our planet may escape being swallowed up, but it will be roasted. The oceans and atmosphere will boil away and life on the planet will be impossible. Farther out in the solar system, the gas giants will shrink as their heated atmospheres escape into space. Life may evolve on newly warmed worlds like Saturn's satellite Titan or Jupiter's moon Europa. But these small bodies will not be able to keep their atmospheres, so life will be very short-lived there.

The Fading of the Sun

After further millions of years, the Sun will become a variable star, flaring and dimming erratically. Then, when the last of its fuel has been exhausted, it will fade and shrink until it is about the size of Earth.

The Earth will become a cold cinder, incapable of supporting life. If human beings have mastered the art of travel to the stars that lie far away in space, they will already have escaped to the planets of some younger star, leaving the solar system behind them.

GLOSSARY

Antimatter Matter composed of atoms in which the electrical charge of the particles is the opposite of those in the corresponding matter.

Asteroid A minor planet, or planetoid. Most move around the Sun between Mars and Jupiter.

Atmosphere A layer of gases surrounding a planet or satellite.

Black hole An extremely dense body in space whose gravity is so strong that nothing, not even light, can escape from it.

Comet A small body consisting of a mixture of rock and ice orbiting the Sun.

Constellations Groups of stars seen from Earth.

Day The time Earth takes to rotate once on its north-south axis. The word is also applied to the time that other planets and satellites take to rotate.

Density The mass of a substance in a given volume. It may be expressed as kilograms per cubic meter (pounds per cubic foot) or in relation to the density of water.

Elliptical Shaped like an ellipse, a closed curve that is a perfect oval. The orbits of the planets and satellites are all elliptical.

Light year The distance that light travels in a year— 9.46 trillion kilometers (5.88 trillion mi).

Magnetic field A place where a magnetic force can be detected.

Mass The amount of matter in an object, measured in kilograms (pounds).

Meteor The phenomenon seen when a meteoroid falls into the Earth's atmosphere and is burned up by the heat generated by friction.

Meteorite A piece of rock sometimes found on the ground after the fall of a meteoroid.

Meteoroid A small piece of rock orbiting the Sun.

Orbit The path of an object around another body— such as a planet around the Sun. The orbits of nearly everything in the solar system are elliptical.

Planet A large body consisting of rock and gas that revolves around a star.

Pressure A measure of the force that presses on a unit area of a substance.

Radiation Any energy that exists in the form of electromagnetic waves (such as light, X rays, radio waves, and microwaves) or streams of particles.

Satellite A small body, natural or artificial, revolving around a planet.

Solar wind Streams of electrically charged particles that flow outward from the Sun.

Star A mass of glowing gas in space, made hot by nuclear reactions.

Year The time that Earth takes to travel around the Sun. The word is also applied to the time that other planets and satellites take to orbit the Sun.

FURTHER INFORMATION

BOOKS TO READ

Bond, Peter. *DK Guide to Space: A Photographic Journey Through the Universe.* DK Publishing, 1999

Graham, Ian. *Astronomy* (Science Spotlight series). Raintree Steck-Vaughn, 1995

Kirkwood, John. *Our Solar System.* Millbrook Press, 1998

Riley, Peter D. *Earth in Space* (Straightforward Science series). Franklin Watts, 1999

WEB SITES

http://cfa-www.harvard.edu
The home page of the Harvard-Smithsonian Center for Astrophysics. Gives information about the center's services and the latest research in astronomy and astrophysics. Provides links to other sources of astronomical information.

http://www.nasa.gov
The home page of NASA. Vast quantities of information about the solar system and human exploration of space.

http://www.seds.org/billa/tnp
The Nine Planets: A Multimedia Tour of the Solar System. A site maintained by Bill Arnett, describing the history, mythology, and current scientific knowledge of each of the planets, moons, and other objects in the solar system.

INDEX

The Universe (30 billion light years across; 1 light year = 9.46 trillion km/5.88 trillion mi)

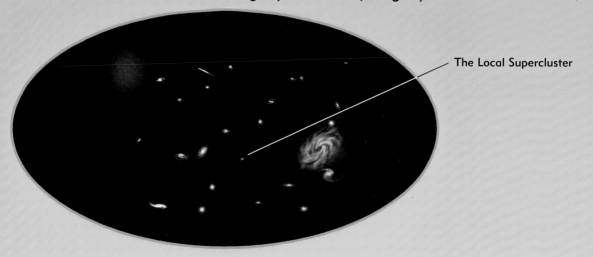

The Local Supercluster

The Local Supercluster (100 million light years across)

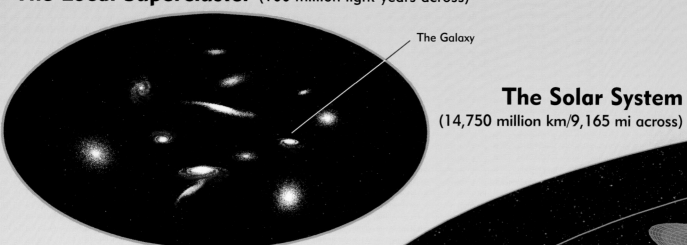

The Galaxy

The Solar System
(14,750 million km/9,165 mi across)

The Galaxy (100,000 light years across)

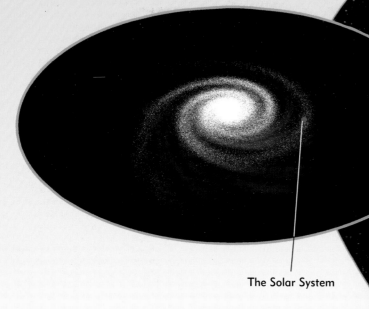

The Solar System

THE SOLAR SYSTEM IN FIGURES

	Distance from Sun (million km/mi)	Diameter at equator (km/mi)	Mass (Earth = 1)	Known moons	Surface gravity (Earth = 1)
1 Sun	–	1,392,000/ 865,000	329,000	–	27.9
2 Mercury	57.9/36	4,878/3,031	0.055	0	0.38
3 Venus	108.2/67	12,104/7,521	0.815	0	0.90
4 Earth	149.6/93	12,756/7,926	1	1	1
5 Mars	227.9/141.6	6,794/4,222	0.11	2	0.38
6 Jupiter	778/484	142,984/88,850	317.8	16	2.6
7 Saturn	1,427/887	120,536/74,901	95.1	19	1.15
8 Uranus	2,870/1,784	51,118/31,765	14.6	17	1.17
9 Neptune	4,497/2,794	50,538/31,404	17.2	8	1.2
10 Pluto	5,900/3,670	2,324/1,444	0.002	1	0.06

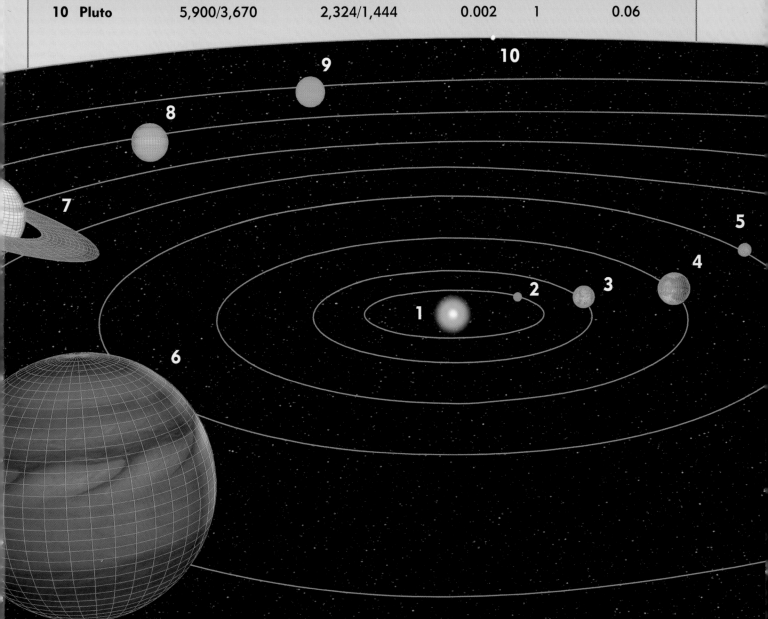